A Pirouette and Gone

E.D. Blodgett

BuschekBooks
Ottawa

*Library and Archives Canada Cataloguing in Publication*

*Blodgett, E. D. (Edward Dickinson), 1935-*
*A pirouette and gone / E.D. Blodgett.*

*ISBN 978-1-894543-60-6*

*1. Children--Poetry. I. Title.*

*PS8553.L56P57 2010 C811'.54 C2010-904865-2*

Cover photography by Yukiko Onley. Used with permission.

Printed in Winnipeg, MB, by Hignell Book Printing.

BuschekBooks, P.O. Box 74053, 5 Beechwood Avenue
Ottawa, Ontario, Canada K1M 2H9
www.buschekbooks.com

BuschekBooks gratefully acknowledges the support of the
Canada Council for the Arts for its publishing program.

 **Canada Council**
**for the Arts**   **Conseil des Arts**
**du Canada**

.

These poems were written especially for

Geoffrey
David
Bronwen
Emily
Charlotte
Sarah
and     Andrew

*Das Kind ist mit jedem Ding vertraut: es ist ihm unmittelbar und in einem Atem doch Gleichnis.*

*Hermann Broch*

Like butterflies their hands
against the setting sun
fly carelessly away

the rain does not come near
their brief fragility
coming and going their flight

without the slightest pause
the air trembles with
the lightness of their wings

o inviolate
the fire invisible
almost igniting grass

impossible to hold
your gaze on them in their
departures into light

At night coyotes cry
the air ringing out
with savage joy and you

suddenly awake
feel their singing run
through your open flesh

its modulations so
swift you have no place
to hide   nothing to know

but how the world leaps
unresistant from
their throats naked and

eternal in the dark
the whimpers that you hear
could not be other than

the world itself in its
uncertain infancy
the childhood of trees

barely standing up
the coldness in the air
the first surprise and last

On all their faces sun
pours down and purposes
of rain that cannot be

unraveled and so their eyes
do not simply see
but take the spectacle

of all falling from air
quietly in to hold
it just as flowers do

but not as flowers they
carry the sun away
joyful thieves that leave

no trace of shame behind
the rain renamed inside
its purpose what they have

of souls and nothing else
to see of them but rain
that has its quietness

laid down upon the ground
of bones unseen as bones
but seen as fountains that

stand forever beneath
a sun that is of them
flinging off their spoils

How his shoulders were
as thin as any stone
worn down beneath the rain

and had you seen him at
a distance in the sun
you would have said he was

a pile of sticks that had
fallen from a nest
of birds during a storm

but here there are no trees
the desert stretches out
of sight against the sky

what to pray that might
in this immensity
be heard where nothing sends

its empty echo back
the stone you thought he seemed
to be so thin it was

a stone that had exhaled
itself to be no more
substantial than a breath

that settles on the ground
no other breath nearby
to draw its being in

No one can count the stars
that circle round their heads
where they are dancing through

the nights across the shore
their steps as intricate
as those of ants at play

and when their feet cross
the steps of other feet
the dance is who they are

and not the dancers they
appear to be before
the dance takes them up

the one body of
the dance a body shared
the cries they think are theirs

composing one song
leaping invisible
into nocturnal air

its one intent to find
the way that leads home
the fragments of their steps

is all that's left of them
the joy that lit the dark
proximities of stars

As if flowers had
suddenly sprung from their
open mouths against

a ground of naked air
and every voice that leapt
surprised into the spring

stood unalloyed before
their faces saying what
it was so swiftly that

the air itself seemed dazed
nothing else was said
in such small mouths

what can words do
but creep into their shade
where roses in their joy

burst all red upon
their lips but in the shape
of red alone and fire

Some were holding out
their hands along the roads
hands no larger than

the leaves that autumn when
the wind has come and gone
abandons to the earth

and from their eyes the light
was scattered   nothing in
its stead but absence that

before the winter comes
and overcomes the sky
their bodies were not seen

nothing of their hands or eyes
was moving in the dust
a prey so easy that

the passing birds refused
and turned gracefully away
gazing at them as

a landscape without depth
where only nothing passed
familiar with the route

Two like birds flew up
and stood upon a branch
a light around them shone

but barely in the dark
and all that could be seen
was that little light

they made upon the branch
and then as one they sang
a small duet that filled

the night around the tree
rising higher through
the branches till it left

the crown behind and reached
yet higher toward the sky
a song that was of them

and solitudes that hung
between the light they were
and darkness and the sky

Just as early rain
with such gentleness
falls upon the roof

their laughter tumbles forth
and irresistible
the music that it makes

so bright you might have thought
that glass would speak so
if its silence broke

and as their mouths against
the sun open with
their sudden cries of joy

their faces all change
flowers take root upon
their tongues where gardens had

not been and paradise
stands up as music then
like falling rain departs

How soon they disappear
the eyes from which the light
in piercing flashes fell

only to return
in memory almost
and seen as they go out

not even stars can take
their likeness on but are
just stars that fall in dark

the eyes that they possessed
float on the tides of blood
and each of them go past

as lanterns in a foreign town
commemorating those
who died in sudden fire

eyes that have become
a story that we tell
ourselves to save the dark

Their eyes float through the smoke
rising from chimneys
high over Europe's plains

not even deer in death
have eyes filled with such
blankness where it is

impossible to find
an end to nothing there
where emptiness

is all that's given back
should they happen to gaze
toward us gazing at them

and in the slightest breeze
no one can discern
a difference between

the smoke and such eyes
that are not capable
to hold us in contempt

perhaps nirvana is
the only gift they have
leaving us with none

And so stately they
walk in twos and threes
unsmiling through your dreams

the language that is theirs
is known only to them
and so subtle that

not a word is said
all their exchanges dance
gracefully from their hands

little changes in
the air that spin around
their bodies' easy pace

and sudden streaks of light
open in their eyes
where all that passes is

taken quickly to heart
there to be carried through
the dark and held as one

might hold in hand a last
breath unbidden that
fell at random there

No more than candles that
sustain the falling of
the night their frailty

is of a majesty
that does not need a crown
nor any other prop

already they have seized
the measure of the moon
among the stars they walk

their hair afloat behind
them lifting as they move
hair that is so fine

it might have been a wake
of spiders hanging in
the early summer air

and hair that if it were
in passing barely touched
would slip unnoticed away

as rays of sun at dusk
that melt into the air
unseen but known   its warmth

placid on the sea
everything held in such
small hands of light

As if for the first time
apple trees upon
the next horizon rise

and all of them begin
to run across the field
their eyes filled with tufts

of flowers just in bloom
and bees from sleep arrive
uncertain where they are

but running down the paths
the children have eyes alone
for flowers hanging like clouds

upon the distant trees
for them alone the trees
exhale the perfect dreams

of apples that their hands
reach up to gather in
the spring passing away

Some seem to forget the steps
that they had learned with such
effort when they began

to stumble across the long
savannahs where they dance
but every step belongs

to what they do so there
is no one who can tell
which step was missed and which

was not as they pass through
the grass and round the stumps
of trees withered away

and all their cries go up
in syncopation with
the jig that they have learned

and when they have returned
as shadows slowly fall
across the huge skies

they prop the little sticks
that they have used for legs
beside the doors that line

the streets and sit without
the least formality
their faces red with joy

as dancers who have turned
so near the stars they seemed
a handsbreadth away

They pressed their faces up
against the windows of
the train going away

their faces seemed to be
masks laid over them
or ghosts of who they were

but ghosts of who they will
become when they rise up
in later memory

they do not know that they
will not be seen again
as they appear now

and if they see at all
it is the rain that runs
along the glass and blurs

their faces and the world
if it were possible
the trees and birds that line

the tracks would howl forth
prophetic cries of pain
the sound of rain would be

lament that falls without
ceasing upon the glass
where they disappear

but all that can be heard
is the engine waning in
the distance till it's gone

they have forgotten how
to cry   the silence in
their eyes the sound of stars

Bearing parasols
above their small heads
against a summer sun

they promenade upon
a shore of infinite
extent in single file

should one begin to sing
another takes it up
until they all with one

song begin to move
in graceful turns beneath
the shade of parasols

from any distance it
could not be said what kind
of creature this might be

this singing dancing shade
whose only life is in
the sun and shade upon

a shore that is not here
but somewhere out of time
where water shyly laps

against their small feet
uncertain what has passed
and birds are held apart

slightly tilting their heads
and so they make their way
through unbelieving afternoons

of falling suns and seas
the traces that they leave
unable to describe

what it could have been
that seemed to happen here
upon a golden shore

How could anyone know
what passed swiftly across
the window-pane and seemed

a shadow or perhaps
the ghost of breath upon
the glass or curtains that

lifted in the wind
but if she sat for more
than instants there to gaze

into the world outside
it was not she we might
have seen sitting there

but solitude itself
that fell upon her like
a long familiar dress

and she had disappeared
invisible inside
it never to be known

as one might gaze into
a window and see inside
nothing but air turned

first to glass and then
lifted into light
the shapes that absence takes

Catching fireflies
their hands stretched out
they run through the night

forgetting what they are
but hands and gleeful cries
escaping from the mouths

and so they pass almost
invisible between
the trees and over fields

until they pass into
the silence and the shade
that will attend them all

and all their movements tend
toward a dance of light
that moves as stars might move

if they were far away
but seemed to be so close
they could be grasped as one

might gather all the light
that lights the universe
in infinitesimal shards

a universe that had
fallen into fragments
just for them to take

and with such sure joy
they enter that expanse
just their hands and cries

Like chickadees they hang
obliquely on the thin
twigs that winter gives

and gaze shyly at us
wondering why we look
at them with such awe

but why do they hang so
flitting from branch to branch
as if to be were just

a moment that without
pausing suddenly leaps
before our eyes and is

displayed in quick cries
nothing can explain
these sudden shifts of light

or that moment of joy
in which they swiftly move
their being that is not

their own as if a hand
had gathered them as one
to hang so before

vanishing among
the trees more memory
than bird or joy or light

Some things failed to fall
into his eager hands
steeples and ships at sea

remained always unknown
except as ships that came
strangely into sight

when stories were told to him
and peaks of mountains that
were lost with skies and cloud

but when he stumbled on
familiarities
of flowers and the grass

what he saw began
to sing behind his eyes
music of the world

as regular as fugues
leaping through his hands
and when he heard the birds

he then began to sing
knowing that so things
are brought to birth upon

the earth as they step forth
from the dark of God's hand
and fall upright in his

Some of them are just
forgotten where they lie
in heaps upon the ground

if you saw them move
you might have said that they
were only playing dead

but no one saw them at all
their faces almost effaced
and no one remembers where

they are along the roads
birds pass over them
and barely see them there

what will cover them
besides the falling rain
in such an emptiness

what tree will give them shade
no prayers are said for them
and no one calls their names

if time were to implode
it would happen here
and nothing but the wind

would carry what was left
of their bare bones
away just as dust

It is not possible
to see at first that they
carry alphabets

in hands that are not large
enough to carry more
or guess what they might spell

rising before their eyes
they see the moon and stars
and cast their letters toward

the sky as if it were
the only prayer they
might think to offer up

as if the stars could not
come into being if
their letters did not stand

beside each other in
the air around them
so spelling the stars

as they were never spelled
before when they were gods
walking there unseen

The moment that he saw
the sun in all its fire
he fell upon the ground

as if all being had
been rapt from what he was
only his body left

if he should cry out
it would be fire that
would leap forth from his mouth

and so he held his hand
before his face appalled
waiting as one who died

and there he lay until
darkness settled on
his unmoving flesh

darkness that was a kind
of coat that one puts on
to save one from the cold

and why the fire did
not take his body then
was not for him to say

or why the dark came down
upon his naked flesh
and kept death from him

but that death had come
he knew and that it was
always near he knew

his body knowing that
darkness in the end
would never be proof

against a sun that was
an immortality
that left none untouched

Some stand up before
us in the darkness of
the longest darkest nights

we think that they are ghosts
that have been torn apart
from immortality

and will like smoke depart
before the first wind
but they do not move

away as we approach
and what we thought was mere
dream begins to stare

at us and stare and stare
their eyes like ours that have
been in the fire and

are eyes that are
impossible to be
more refined and more

unwavering in their
coming in to us
like meteors that have

nowhere in the world
to fall but in the soil
we give up to them

Some were taken so
swiftly they did not know
where they had been if they

had been at all with us
some were taken up
by fire some by stone

and some by steel that left
them lying broken on
the ground where they had walked

no one believes that this
could be the way that such
small beings leave the world

and in the darkness stones
are heard to cry and stars
and nothing in between

Each of them thought that they
had formed a  row of trees
that stood beside a road

they merely had to start
by holding their arms out straight
and stare at nothing at all

the world emptied before
their eyes until the sun
and sky had disappeared

they stood this way for years
one day soldiers walked
beneath them and thought that they

were beautiful and old
they hung their prisoners
from branches above the road

after they had left
the trees opened their eyes
death hung from their arms

they saw the sky again
and saw the sun was dark
and thought that they were blind

now they carry death
along the quiet roads
and have no place to go

Some believe they will
return from death like flocks
of doves wheeling above

the roofs to find their nests
and on their skin the air
will take them into warmth

the air will seem to be
a second womb but so
large that no outside

is possible to know
and through the night they will
keep murmuring among

themselves so that the air
will seem to be but them
and their reports of what

they may have been before
death came over them
and they were lifted to

the sky to turn against
the sun that stands on its
horizons waiting for

night to come at last
to hold their whispers of
what they thought they were

Some do not seem to see
that war has passed their way
and where their houses stood

nothing appears instead
where fire was and steel
and through remains they run

their laughter filling the air
with echoes of the games
that always had been theirs

but they have souls that walk
slower and slower through
the spaces that were streets

and gaze at what had been
a world with large eyes
like bees that have been caught

in amber silence where
eternity is all
the time that they possess

At first no one knew
if they were dancing to
a pattern they had learned

but when they turned it seemed
that they were birds that were
returning in the spring

then suddenly it was
autumn horizons that
appeared bearing the moon

and sometimes as they leaned
it seemed a tiger asleep
as all their feet stood poised

no one could explain
the metamorphoses
their dancing had become

except to think it was
what could arise alone
from their fragile bones

that moved in them as if
they were birds that were
only at home in flight

and had without the least
knowledge fallen from
a kabbalah that springs

to life when they begin
to dance across the place
that holds the heart of God

Their departures are
more unbearable
than any that are known

when they enter the world
an apocalypse
unfolds and then stands up

it is the last of things
but in reverse so that
in them the stars are new

their brightness in our eyes
seems as if it were
unremembered till

that moment when they draw
breath and make their first
sound against the air

to see them suddenly
depart in silence toward
the dark is nothing else

but knowing that the sun
has lost the power to
return and what is left

but knowledge that has not
the light to know what it
had known before they left

Their voices could be heard
singing before they came
visible on the roads

none of the words were clear
but just the syllables
that floated in the air

no bells could leave such light
traces along the air
their music coming down

nor could the merest rain
fall so absently
that when it has passed by

it is not sure that it
has been present at all
and when their echo

is no longer heard
it is not possible
to say if they had passed

the only knowledge of
their being in the air
a longing that descends

upon the roads unseen
and sits quietly down
unsure where it can go

Some lay on the ground
moving their arms and legs
to make angels of

the snow that lies beneath
a shell of holiness
that takes their bodies in

and stillness slowly breathes
upon the shape they share
knowing in their bones

that so eternity
moves at random here
and there beneath the sun

walking away they spare
a glance against the ground
where their bodies lay

no questions form inside
their minds as they behold
the look that angels have

assuming shadows to
be everywhere that they
have moved across the earth

where they have left themselves
in brief memorials
that disappear without

the slightest trace that words
might leave or other signs
a pirouette and gone

Certain mornings are
so clear they seem to have
fallen from the south

no one remembers rain
only a kind of light
that penetrates the stones

unconcerned they walk
into the light and it
in turn passes through

the bright transparency
of their open flesh
so exposed they are

and when it enters them
their bodies stream fire
and as the night descends

they exhale the dark
the stars forming upon
the heaven of their flesh

birds keening with song
hover in their breath
the clarity that air

possesses standing up
inside them and rings out
as if the sabbath was

the burden of their hands
apocalypse without
remembrance on their skin

After echoes of
their voices fill their ears
they do not know where they

should put their hands unless
it is just at their sides
as if to keep themselves

from losing balance now
that their voices are all
around them in the air

where they cannot be seen
but all the sounds that leap
unbidden from their mouths

are now repeating them
like shadows that are not
attached to them but free

a music unpossessed
that gives them silences
that now become known

as only silence is
when it appears from what
is absolute in its

being not all
but something after that
music carries in

its wake that seems to stand
at first unnoticed then
takes shape like eyes that close

They stepped uncertain in
the snow that stretched before
them to the world's end

its whiteness was all that they
could see and in their minds
all that had been was gone

every step they took
was one that no one had
ventured to take before

they had no words for this
where all that lay behind
and all after was blank

except where steps were seen
that marked their presence there
late in the afternoon

before they entered night
they saw its surface had
changed to pale blue

all the eternity
they were to have was here
their steps going round

the light so radiant
the shadows that were theirs
stretched out behind them on

the snow as if the light
had fallen in patches that
were bright and pale and still

Sometimes beyond all
hearing the music that
they make comes into

the world as they are seen
skating on a pond
against a winter moon

near the edges reeds
stand up and shiver in
the wind against the snow

but of them all
that can be seen are brief
explosions of what

they wear weaving across
the pond in circles that
break and form and break

all the being they
possess is there in that
music they make as one

against the moon at night
colours going off
unechoed through the air

A girl was singing through
the night in solitude
keeping the stars where they

were placed until they fell
away into the dark
her voice so clear that clouds

could not bear to be clouds
longer and disappeared
and when the moon rose

into the air of night
her voice sprang up to meet
the blessing it bestowed

and sang more clearly still
as if the moon were her
singular audience

and as her singing rose
she paused from time to time
hearing filling her face

and then her song resumed
a song that had become
a song for two at night

one voice for the moon
the other for the girl
each of them aware

there was no other thing
for them to do but sing
across their solitudes

the night their only stage
where brightness rose and fell
through the air they shared

Nothing more than a
departing whisper in
the deeper leaves as if

it were a breeze that paused
or birds that disappeared
too soon to be observed

so are their eyes inside
the world that seem to look
and quickly look away

noticed only as
a light that has gone out
all timidity

briefly proffered and
withdrawn riffling apart
and so at night it is

uncertain if their eyes
rise up in dreams or if
they are everywhere

like distant ships that pass
below horizons where
their lights were seen perhaps

or only thought they were
the air suddenly left
chill and turning dark

Their bodies are so brief
arcing in the sun
between water and air

and when they strike the sea
nothing resists the small
force that they possess

water air and light
explode upon themselves
as glass will fly apart

no centre lies inside
the light embracing them
and moving without hands

nor can gravity
explain what now can be
the keeping of the day

how else are they but as
ghosts returning to stand
radiant from the play

of forces that contend
streaming over them
indistinguishable

from other elements
and walk along the shore
the day in them on fire

They carry candles through
the early evening dusk
their faces grave against

the deepening layers of
the night that settles on
their slowly moving frames

they walk across a field
no one leading them
and come upon a wood

without pausing they step
inside and disappear
the songs that follow them

hang above the field
hesitantly like birds
that have lost their way

and try a song and then
one more before the sun
departs into the night

and through the silent wood
only the small flames
continue on their way

as if fireflies
had formed into a flock
smaller and smaller until

the light they carried was
no more than memory
that passes fitful through

the mind where stars appear
to take their place against
the coming of the night

They formed a circle on
a plain and all that was
above turned with them

and in their centre stood
a small and leafless tree
to tell them where they were

all that they might know
of mere eternity
they knew upon their flesh

but it was flesh that seemed
transparent in the light
and all that was above

sun and moon and stars
turned around with them
and turning sent their light

through their bodies till
they seemed but outlines of
figures on a plain

so when dark came down
upon them in the night
only their eyes remained

visible with light
as they danced round and round
the little tree that had

disappeared from sight
only their eyes left
to know where the world was

or who they were when they
had lost their silhouettes
and when beside the light

the wind passed through them as
they turned beneath the stars
the centre in their eyes

One day they gave up
playing dead to play
apocalypse instead

and when the sun began
to set slowly against
the western edge of the world

so huge and round and red
they walked beside it one
after another and then

stepped off into the air
all of them began
to sing the song that they

loved more than any of
the other songs they knew
and so they filled the air

with an infinity of songs
following the sun
in all its circuits through

the bright melodic air
the temper of their songs
taking holiness

into their burning mouths
to pour it forth transformed
sustaining the farthest star

How calm the sea when they
saw it for the first time
and unafraid they thought

it was a country that
must be the mirror of
their own where they as in

a glass reflected walked
as they walked there along
the shore beneath the moon

but those upon the sea
seemed unable to speak
as silent as the stars

that lay before them on
the water's surface where they
looked back into the light

which seemed to be their home
and looking from the shore
they thought they saw their souls

afloat before them on
the sea where silence was
all that they could hear

and smaller lights that shone
farther out where the
horizon fades into sky

Music seems nearer them
than breath and hearing it
they cannot help but leap

toward it in their delight
feet in the air and hands
desiring to take it in

and so they dance beside
stones unable to
stand up and follow them

yet in silence they
move on in mystery
so music is not all

but what they hear inside
the punctuated air
being itself inhaled

as if music were
a flower that set forth
its blossoms through the air

and breathing it they breathe
all that they can be
joy is what they exhale

when they exhale themselves
the flower given back
and music and the dance

how they open their hands
all the taking in
the one gift that is theirs

Unnoticed loneliness
slipped through her like a stone
and settled near her heart

it was a stone that rain
had made so smooth that if
she touched it anywhere

she could not have said
if it were more than air
that she had in her hands

but nothing could remove
its immeasurable weight
where it unmoving seemed

to fall through all the space
that floated round her heart
as if she were great

with gravity and death
around it a cosmos could
take shape where nothing would

reside and moons pass by
without the least light
and stars that were not known

One season was theirs
and it was summer when
the sun lay late upon

their cheeks and golden hair
their eyes shining with
the early evening light

how still they stood upon
a narrow field that stretched
before them like a stream

where they floated away
like lanterns set afire
to remember them

who had already gone
apart on fire too
their faces glowing in dark

farther and farther away
coming upon a sea
that was infinity

for them and there almost
out of sight they stood
against the night sky

appearing smaller than
bobbing fireflies
then the curtain of

the sky passed over them
nothing in the air
but distant sighs of streams

There was a sound inside
a box that only birds
can make when they are small

abandoned birds that have
no strength to think they will
be found or heard or known

children in the trains
left at stations must
have made a sound like that

and sounds of scratching that
became part of the wood
of which the cars were made

after the cars had left
it was not long before
they came back again

there was no echo in
the air of crying left
just the stubborn sound

carried by the cars
of something in the wood
invisible and yet

plainly heard of small
fingers that never cease
the music that they made

was made of silence that
is of birds when they
have no more sound to make

They stood beside a lake
before the sun had set
gazing at themselves

and saw how their faces
looked back at them almost
as in a mirror but

a mirror that allowed
spaces of water to
enter them so that

they seemed smaller and
scattered in pieces across
the surface of the pond

they did not believe that this
was what they were but knew
that they were somewhere there

and when darkness fell
they saw that they were gone
and in their place they saw

the stars that danced across
the pond where they had been
stars that were alive

like they and giving off
the light that they had seen
coming from their eyes

the sky darker but
the same where they had been
kinship was enough

and they did not move
but stood and saw the stars
float in the night and them

For some the world was
not possible to see
and flowers that they knew

rose up invisible
and soft inside their hands
each petal known

by how their fingers moved
across the faces turned
unseeing in toward them

they knew the sun had set
when all the sounds around
their heads grew quieter

and other sounds sprang up
beating along the ground
and running to their feet

and death they knew when they
took silence like a ball
of no silence they had

heard into their hands
and it did not depart
then it was they heard

the silence that was theirs
that had no echo but
what their flesh gives up

Her voice rose up into
the quiet air and if
snow had fallen there

it would have seemed almost
as pure as what was heard
and suddenly it stopped

as snow too might stop
before it comes to rest
upon the ground where ghosts

of snow hover unsure
where they have now arrived
the silence that remains

cannot be more steeped
in purity than this
no image of the girl

taking shape and no
echo that would
bring her presence back

even the trees have lost
their weight against the air
the going out of snow

They came into the room
like moments after rain
has fallen and a breeze

springs up within the leaves
then disappears and leaves
stillness in its wake

they do not open their mouths
all that they desire
to say is spoken by

the light that fills their eyes
without the benefit
of sun and where the smoke

of ruined buildings turns
and if screams are heard
they fall as darkness falls

gently and without
a sound against the day
nothing else appears

to take shape in their eyes
and if there are tears
it is how rain returns

to memory where rain
rarely falls before
it turns again to air

When they awoke they knew
that they were apples that
were hanging on a tree

apples that had just
begun to take shape
their skins turning red

beneath the sun and rain
and hanging there they knew
the mystery of fruit

rising from flowers that
are dreams that trees possess
dreams that open and

without a murmur give
themselves slowly away
to be the apples that

their waking is for trees
autumn having no
sweeter sound than how

they quietly strike the ground
when winter and the moon
are in the night air

and falling they return
to sleep as if it were
for them the deeper fruit

They sat upon a floor
holding dolls in their laps
the floor seemed broader than

any floor they knew
and with them on the floor
they saw besides the stars

showers far away
come and go without
any sound at all

as if they feared their dolls
might suddenly leap into
the night to float among

the stars and passing rain
they held them closer in
their arms where they might be

the thing that held them where
they had been put beside
the night and stars and rain

the thing that saw them through
the eyes that could not see
and hands that could not know

the fear that lay upon
their flesh where they sat on
a floor awake where if

infinity had walked
it would have moved without
the slightest echo heard

Now they are gone to smoke
the voices that once rang out
like bells across the fields

the light that lay upon
their skin at evening
the moment that their feet

touched the ground when they
would hear music move
suddenly through their bones

all so swiftly dissolved
and nothing passing through
the air but wisps of smoke

a countryside that is
too serene to be
awakened from its sleep

where birds among the trees
without expression gaze
at smoke unmoved to sing

Their traces on water are
no deeper than what trees
might leave if there were sun

it was a stream where they
would come at first light
to see the faces there

come in sight and then
depart as if they were
what always flowed past

pausing briefly for them
and when they came no more
something in the stream

grew darker where the shade
never came near it from
the darkness of the shore

if the rain should fall
the stream is barely touched
the circles that it leaves

slipping away into
the slow embrace of dark
the memory of trees

the stones along the shore
the wind that passed above
unable to be borne

When least expected then
they are alive against
the sun and moon and stars

and all gravity
taken from their flesh
they do not walk but dance

their bodies poised to hold
the clarity of light
that pours over them

what if they should speak
how the air would seem
to turn to crystal then

and if they lift their hands
trees would take shape
and grass would spring from earth

genesis is in
no other place but where
they have chosen to walk

unable to occur
without the least smile
and then the stars fall

They stepped without an end
in mind upon the earth
and all the silence that

the earth possessed rose up
and passed into their bones
and so the silence they

carried with them where
they walked was part of that
greater silence of

the earth and stones and grass
nothing else explains
the grace that circles them

and when it is their turn
to sleep upon the ground
the stars when they appear

turn slowly in their hands
the night enclosing them
their eternity

can take no other shape
their little bodies turned
to hold a universe

that turns in them unseen
waking or sleeping or
being where silence comes

How to tell the way
they go when they depart
is it light that fails

or is it darkness that
fills the air without
anyone taking note

but when they can be seen
no more in any place
their absence then is more

than what they were when seen
and seems to draw the air
down close to the ground

the darkness of the night
putting out the stars
nothing can be heard

but the silence of
the stones and grass and dirt
fragments of the sun

fall inconsolate
from heaven down without
awareness what they touch

And so clean were their eyes
they might when first beheld
seem invisible

except for unknown birds
who saw that they were lakes
that open by themselves

without the need for rain
and stand nowhere but in
the still air of night

they see them by the stars
that find in them a new
heaven where they might rise

but seeing in them shapes
never appearing before
as of mythologies

waiting to be composed
and so they knew that this
was where their journeys through

the deeper reaches of
the air had taken them
and if their end had come

it was to stand beside
this place that did not move
and where in darkness stars

that were before unknown
rising beneath their feet
arose and stopped and shone

When music entered them
they each stood up as tall
as they imagined that

they could if they stood up
and reached above their heads
and so they thought themselves

as elms that rose against
the moon on summer nights
their branches touching stars

it seemed as if their eyes
had disappeared into
their dream to reach the sky

but when beneath the dark
the wind passed through their leaves
the world they could not see

was filled with music that
the air that fell upon
them from the heavens made

nothing that they did
could make music so
just the universe

that entered them and so
changed that no one knew
that if the moon spoke

this was how it would
explain its passage there
where they merely exhaled

She wanted to raise her arm
to recognize the sun
to greet the passing birds

but she had lost her arm
and so invisibly
she raised it nonetheless

could it be that they
the sun and passing birds
saw what none could see

they were not heard to weep
but possibly they cried
aloud where beauty stood

so firmly in their eyes
her face full of the sun
and ears more deeply filled

with songs of passing birds
and for a moment no
being other than

these could be the world
held in one embrace
of praise invisible

Her face was nothing more
than a page torn from a book
that in the evening wind

might be seen to be
moving from street to street
as if she were a dream

from which one could not wake
and other children ran
behind her hoping they

might take her in their hands
and hold her as a prize
that they triumphantly

hold up for all to see
as a divinity
and while they ran they did

not notice how they too
had entered in the dream
not seeing how the wind

kept lifting up her face
not seeing that there was
nothing to see behind

her face but evening and
the wind that offered her
to their desire that

filled them running through
the night much closer to
the darkness than they knew

Nothing keeps them from
their love of smallest things
the early grass and stones

they see beside the roads
a wind of ecstasy
blows through them then and they

have no desire but
to be in turn the grass
the stones that shine in the sun

and so their stepping forth
into the spring is in
the form of prayers that

whisper into the air
and given to the birds
who take upon themselves

the task of lifting what
they say and casting it
like seeds across the earth

as if they knew that these
were syllables that held
all the sense there is

echoes of the wind
that barely open where
silence falls as rain

Like little soldiers they
marched along the road
their hands were beautiful

shining in the sun
and eyes and all their flesh
joy from their bodies burst

no line can form between
their bodies and their souls
and only suns possess

such plenitude
its light the light that flows
from them enough to be

almost too bright to know
and so they all went by
one by one to death

their bodies long farewells
of immortality
that set like small suns

For just an instant they
paused above the blue
waters of the lake

the instant passed and so
did they and all that was
above the lake was sky

but in that moment there
was no greater joy
as if it were the world

and not they which brought
such ecstasy into
the air for instants that

touched eternity
and when it was they fell
the eternal fell

with them but fell inside
itself where joy lies stored
to be born again

in them as they leap forth
from it and into it
falling to water then

When they were finished they
were seen standing in
the windows where the light

came down in such a way
that they were hard to see
but in the light their hands

were moving to and fro
no way to tell if they
were signalling goodbye

or simply recognizing
what went past outside
no deeper than the glass

where they were partly to
be seen within the light
already growing dim

nothing touches them
the one shadow that
appears to grow across

the glass and makes their hands
appear less and less
like hands that trace their small

arcs diminishing
like butterflies within
their immortality